Festivals

LEVEL 10

DECODABLES BY jump!

Teaching Tips

White Level 10
This book focuses on developing reading independence, fluency, and comprehension.

Before Reading
- Ask readers what they think the book will be about based on the title. Have them support their answer.

Read the Book
- Encourage readers to read silently on their own.
- As readers encounter unfamiliar words, ask them to look for context clues to see if they can figure out what the words mean. Encourage them to locate boldfaced words in the glossary and ask questions to clarify the meaning of new vocabulary.
- Allow readers time to absorb the text and think about each chapter.
- Ask readers to write down any questions they have about the book's content.

After Reading
- Ask readers to summarize the book.
- Encourage them to point out anything they did not understand and ask questions.
- Ask readers to review the questions on page 23. Have them go back through the book to find answers. Have them write their answers on a separate sheet of paper.

© 2024 Booklife Publishing
This edition is published by arrangement with Booklife Publishing.

North American adaptations © 2024 Jump!
5357 Penn Avenue South
Minneapolis, MN 55419
www.jumplibrary.com

Decodables by Jump! are published by Jump! Library.
All rights reserved. No part of this book may be reproduced in any form without written permission from the publisher.

Library of Congress Cataloging-in-Publication Data is available at www.loc.gov or upon request from the publisher.

ISBN: 979-8-88524-805-1 (hardcover)
ISBN: 979-8-88524-806-8 (paperback)
ISBN: 979-8-88524-807-5 (ebook)

Photo Credits

Images are courtesy of Shutterstock.com. With thanks to Getty Images, Thinkstock Photo and iStockphoto. Cover – StockImageFactory.com. p4–5 – Aliii, Anel Alijagic. p6–7 – Sarath maroli, Mohamed Reedi. p8–9 – Anneka, Jonathan Hudson. p10–11 – Vietnam Stock Images, Nattapoom V. p12–13 – marino bocelli. p14–15 – Noam Armonn, Yitz Fisch. p16–17 – StockImageFactory.com, Prabhjit S. Kalsi. p18–19 – wavebreakmedia, Pixel-Shot. p20–21 – TTLSC, Jaba.

Table of Contents

Page 4   Festivals and Celebrations

Page 6   Muslim Festivals

Page 8   Christian Festivals

Page 10   Buddhist Festivals

Page 12   Sikh Festivals

Page 14   Jewish Festivals

Page 16   Hindu Festivals

Page 18   Secular Festivals

Page 20   New Year's Festivals

Page 22   Index

Page 23   Questions

Page 24   Glossary

Festivals and Celebrations

Festivals are events during which communities celebrate together. Festivals can celebrate happy events, such as a day that is important to a country. Festivals can also celebrate days that are special to a religion.

Many festivals are celebrated with fireworks.

Many people follow a religion. A religion is a shared set of beliefs and ideas about people and their relationship to a god or gods. Some of the most-practiced religions are:

- Islam
- Christianity
- Buddhism
- Sikhism
- Judaism
- Hinduism

Festivals can be celebrated with special food, music, decorations, and **traditions**.

Muslim Festivals

Ramadan and Eid-al Fitr

During Ramadan, Muslim adults **fast** by not eating during the day. They spend time praying and doing good deeds. People thank Allah for helping them be strong through fasting. Special prayers are said at mosques.

Ramadan ends with the festival of Eid-al Fitr. Delicious foods are eaten.

Eid al-Adha

Muslims try to make a **pilgrimage** to Mecca at least once. Mecca is the Muslim holy city. Eid al-Adha is a festival at the end of the pilgrimage.

Millions of people go to Mecca every year.

Muslims go to a mosque for special prayers at Eid al-Adha. It is a time to visit family and friends and do good deeds.

Christian Festivals

Christmas

Christmas celebrates the birth of Jesus Christ. The Christmas story tells us how Mary and Joseph traveled on a donkey to Bethlehem. In Bethlehem, Mary gave birth to Jesus, the son of God. Angels brought the good news of his birth to some shepherds. Wise Men visited Jesus and brought gifts.

Easter

Easter is the most important festival to Christians. This festival celebrates the **resurrection** of Jesus Christ. On Good Friday, Christians remember the day of Jesus's death on the cross. On Easter Sunday, Christians remember the day Jesus rose from the **tomb**, three days after his death.

Buddhist Festivals

Vesak

Vesak is a festival that celebrates Buddha's birth. Before he was known as Buddha, he was called Siddhartha Gautama. He chose not to be a prince and became Buddha instead. On Vesak Day, Buddhists celebrate by doing good deeds and going to the temple.

Some Buddhists celebrate Vesak with lantern decorations.

Dharma Day

Some Buddhists celebrate Dharma Day to remember when Buddha began sharing his teachings. Buddha is an important person to Buddhist people. Dharma Day is spent listening to talks and reading from Buddhist scriptures. Dharma Day can be celebrated in a temple or a monastery.

Sikh Festivals

Vaisakhi

Vaisakhi celebrates the beginning of the Sikh community in 1699. The Sikh place of **worship** is called a Gurdwara, and it is decorated for Vaisakhi. There are parades, called Nagar Kirtan, and special food. The parades are led by people in traditional clothing.

The Nagar Kirtan are very colorful and exciting!

Bandi Chhor Divas

Bandi Chhor Divas is a festival of lights. It celebrates the time the Guru Hargobind saved 52 princes from prison. The emperor would only free the men that could hold onto his coat. The Guru made a special coat with 52 tassels for them to hold, so the princes all went free.

Jewish Festivals

Passover

Passover remembers the Jews being led out of Egypt to freedom by Moses. This is known as the Exodus. The festival begins with a Seder—a special meal with prayers and **rituals** to help tell the Exodus story. The Seder has special foods which represent the Exodus story.

The Seder meal

Hanukkah

Hanukkah tells the story of the Jewish people fighting to defend their right to believe in God. After the fight, they lit their special lamp, called a menorah, but they only had a tiny bit of oil left. By a miracle, the tiny bit of oil burned for eight days!

Hanukkah lasts for eight days.

Hindu Festivals

Diwali

Diwali is the Hindu festival of lights. It lasts for five days. Diwali celebrates the story of how Prince Rama rescued Princess Sita from the evil king, Ravana. He was helped by Hanuman, the monkey god. The people lit a row of lamps to help them get home again.

Holi

Hindus celebrate the triumph of good over evil during Holi. The Holi story tells us how Prahlad worshipped the Hindu god Vishnu and not his father, an evil king. The king's sister Holika tricked Prahlad into sitting in a fire with her, but Prahlad was protected!

People light bonfires and throw colorful powders into the air to celebrate Holi.

Secular Festivals

People who are not religious also like to celebrate. Many festivals are not religious at all. Some countries remember the end of wars with celebrations, sometimes for hundreds of years after. Others have national days that mark their **independence** or celebrate their country.

The 4th of July marks the day the United States became its own country.

Festivals that are not based on a religion are called secular festivals. Some festivals are both religious and secular or have become more secular over time. For example, Christmas is an important festival to Christians, but many things we do at Christmas are not religious at all.

New Year's Festivals

Much of the western world celebrates New Year's Day on January 1, marking the day the year changes. There are often fireworks, celebrations, and street parties. New Year's Day is a hopeful time to look back at the year that has passed and forward to the year ahead.

Some parts of the world celebrate the new year differently. The Jewish festival of Rosh Hashanah celebrates the new year over two days in fall.

Chinese New Year falls between January 21 and February 20. Chinese New Year has a story about a monster named Nian.

Index

fireworks 4, 20
gods 5, 8, 15–17
lights 13, 16–17
prayers 6–7, 14
princes 13, 16

secular 19
stories 8, 14–17, 21

How to Use an Index

An index helps us find information in a book. Each word has a set of page numbers. These page numbers are where you can find information about that word.

Example: balloons 5, 8–10, 19

Important word

Page numbers

This means page 8, page 10, and all the pages in between.
Here, it means pages 8, 9, and 10.

Questions

1. What is a secular festival?

2. How long does the oil burn for in the Jewish story of Hanukkah?

3. What do people throw on Holi?

4. Can you use the Table of Contents to find information about Chinese New Year?

5. Can you use the Index to find information about princes?

6. Using the Glossary, can you define what traditions are?

Glossary

fast:
To stop drinking and eating for a time.

independence:
Freedom.

pilgrimage:
A journey taken for religious reasons.

resurrection:
The act of rising from the dead.

rituals:
Acts or series of acts that are always performed in the same way.

tomb:
A grave, room, or building that holds a dead body.

traditions:
Customs, ideas, or beliefs that are handed down from one generation to the next.

worship:
To show love and devotion to a god, especially by praying or going to a religious service.